ADVANCED CONTEST SOLOS
FOR CLARINET

VOLUME 1

To access audio visit:
www.halleonard.com/mylibrary

Enter Code
5022-9614-0065-8270

ISBN 978-1-59615-252-6

MMO Music Minus One

EXCLUSIVELY DISTRIBUTED BY

HAL•LEONARD®

7777 W. BLUEMOUND RD. P.O. BOX 13819 MILWAUKEE, WI 53213

Visit Hal Leonard Online at
www.halleonard.com

CONTENTS

PERFORMANCE GUIDE

BRAHMS
Sonata in F Minor, Op. 120, No. 1
4th Movement: Vivace

This is probably one of the most popular works of its kind. You will need to listen to and study the piano part. (It is wrong to refer to the piano part as an "accompaniment" in this type of music!) Chamber music demands an equal collaboration between players. Brahms indicated exactly what he wanted, so be careful to observe all the indications in the score. This piece is beautifully written with much contrast between sustained and detached sections.

The Vivace begins with a statement of the theme by the piano. The clarinet has fragments of this theme (see measure 32) but doesn't play the whole subject until measure 174. Notice the interplay of the second theme. The clarinet first takes this theme in measure 9, with eighth note pick-ups in the previous bar. In measure 109, the piano has the theme in parallel sixths while the clarinet accompanies with an Alberti figure. It will be most helpful if you study the score to see how Brahms uses his fine melodies. The quarter note triplets beginning in measure 42 should not be difficult if you remember that the melodic interest is in the piano part until measure 46, when both instruments join together in a sweeping *dolce.* A brilliant conversation begins in measure 54, with the piano making a statement and the clarinet imitating later, but in the same bar. Listen carefully to the piano, and try to reproduce every nuance!

New material is introduced by the piano in measure 119. When the clarinet enters in measure 123, you will want a gentle tone and a simple, straight forward approach. The repeated G naturals in the section beginning with measure 142 are merely an harmonic accompaniment; be sure to blend with the piano. The clarinet plays another fragment of the first theme in measures 207 through 210, and the piece finishes with brilliant arpeggios.

HINDEMITH
Sonate
2nd Movement: Lebhaft

The Hindemith Sonate is one of the most played modern pieces for clarinet, especially popular with college students. Mr. Hindemith was a master composer who provided sonatas for many different instruments. It was my good fortune to perform and record chamber music with him. He had a tremendous knowledge, and his music lies beautifully for the clarinet.

The little sixteenth note figures must be played evenly. Be careful to follow the articulation indicated by the composer. Notice how legato passages are interspersed with detached sections. The relationship between the piano and the clarinet is very tight. Compare the piano part in measures 5 and 6 with the clarinet part in measures 30 and 31!

Watch your rhythm in measure 77. Don't let the second group of sixteenth notes take you by surprise. The phrase beginning with the pick-up to measure 91 is a condensation of material used at the beginning. This is an example of the diversity possible through economical means!

HINDEMITH
Sonate
4th Movement: Kleines Rondo, gemachlich

The composer takes the main theme of this "Little Rondo" through many key changes. Compare the opening statement with the episode beginning in measure 16:

You will have a better understanding of this music if you locate all the statements of this theme. The second theme, much more lyric in character, is stated first in measure 24:

A little study will enable you to differentiate between these themes. The smooth *legato* of the second theme contrasts nicely with the more abrupt mood of the first theme. When the composer combines the two themes, as he does in the development, you can show the structure of the piece through dynamic changes and variations in your articulation.

MOZART
Concerto, K. 622
Rondo

Mozart wrote this Concerto for Anton Stadler, a famous clarinetist of his day. The Rondo is cheerful and sprightly, and demands a bright, light tone. The rhythm must be precise. You will need to be especially careful to give those phrases ending in eighth notes their full value. It is a temptation to cut phrases too short, when they end in eighth notes followed by rests. Study the following phrase:

Mozart did not indicate articulation in his original score. You should feel free to choose whatever approach you prefer, providing it is suitable to the classic style. The section beginning with the pick-up to measure 138 is very lyric. You will need to work for a smooth legato in this episode.

Measure 169 is sometimes played in the upper octave:

This seems very logical, since the other portions of this sequence (in measures 171 and 173) are also on the staff. The many scales and arpeggios must not sound like exercises. You might *crescendo* the ascending passages, and *decrescendo* those passages which descend. Breathing should not offer any special difficulties. Mozart's writing is so logical that with a little practice, this Rondo should "play itself!"

SONATA IN F MINOR

IV

JOHANNES BRAHMS
Arr. by Alamiro Giampieri

♩ = 88 (5'09")

3225

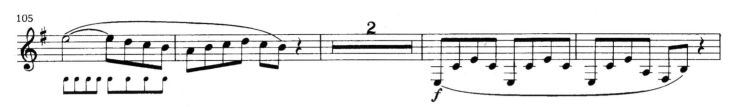

3225

SONATE

II

PAUL HINDEMITH

3225

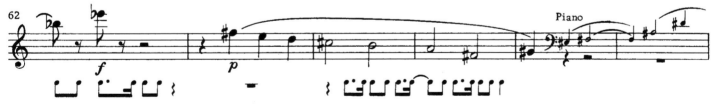

3225

♩ = 88 (2'38")

PAUL HINDEMITH

Kleines Rondo, gemachlich

CONCERTO, K.622

Rondo

WOLFGANG A. MOZART
Revised by Erich Simon

3225

cresc.

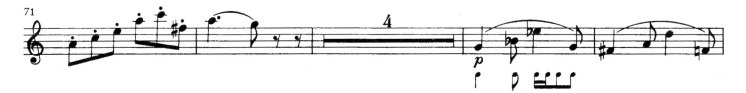

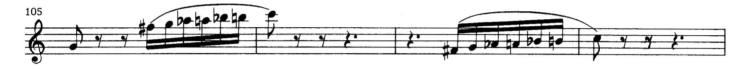

159

164

169

174

cresc.

178

184

190

194

200

207

3225

3225

BEETHOVEN – PIANO QUINTET IN E-FLAT MAJOR, OP. 16

The E-flat Beethoven quintet is a wonderful example of Beethoven at his best. Beautiful sonorities in one of the great classics of chamber music. The Andante is especially beautiful, with an almost perfect integration of all the instruments.

Performed by The New Art Wind Quintet
Accompaniment: Harriet Wingreen, piano
00190525 Book/CD Pack $14.99

BRAHMS – CLARINET QUINTET IN B MINOR, OP. 115

Brahms' magnificent B-minor Clarinet Quintet is one of the summits of the chamber repertoire for clarinet. It is in many ways an homage to Mozart's classic quintet for clarinet. Not to be overlooked by any serious clarinetist. This deluxe set includes the quintet in its original key with printed parts for both A and B-flat clarinets, and adds a repitched version for B-flat clarinetists, allowing players of that instrument to learn the same fingerings as the composer's intended A clarinet for performance purposes. Includes a high-quality, newly engraved printed music score with parts in the original key for both A clarinet and B-flat clarinets; plus online audio with a complete recording of the quintet, with soloist; and a second performance minus the soloist. Also includes audio featuring a recording of the quintet repitched to allow B-flat clarinetists to play the original written part for A-clarinet.

Performed by Collete Galante, clarinet • Accompaniment: The Classic String Quartet
00400323 Book/Online Audio $19.99

BRAHMS – SONATAS IN F MINOR AND E-FLAT, OP. 120

Favorites of clarinetists and pinnacles of the repertoire, these two sonatas are always popular on recital programs everywhere. Hear the piece performed by American virtuoso Jerome Bunke, then you play them again with his accompanist. Presented here in the original key with printed parts for B-flat clarinets, this 2-CD set includes complete reference performance, piano accompaniments, plus a slow-tempo practice version of the accompaniments to help you as you learn the piece!

Performed by Jerome Bunke, clarinet
Accompaniment: Hidemitsu Hayashi, piano
00400046 Book/2-CD Pack................................. $19.99

CLARINET CAMEOS – CLASSIC CONCERT PIECES FOR CLARINET AND ORCHESTRA

This album of magnificent concert-pieces hails from the greatest works in musical history. Includes the finest concert pieces, beautifully arranged for clarinet and orchestra, ranging from Bach's masterful 'Air on a G String' to the long, romantic melodic lines of the Berceuse from 'Jocelyn,' or Beethoven's sprightly Minuet in G. The nine pieces presented in this MMO edition, intended for instrumentalists of intermediate-to-advanced level, are material that any clarinetist will cherish forever. Virtuoso clarinetist Anton Hollich performs these masterpieces with the Stuttgart Symphony Orchestra, then you take center-stage under the baton of Maestro Emil Kahn. An exciting and rewarding collection for performer and audience alike!

Performed by Anton Hollich, clarinet
Accompaniment: Stuttgart Symphony Orchestra
Conductor: Emil Kahn
00400106 Book/CD Pack $14.99

MOZART – PIANO QUINTET IN E-FLAT MAJOR, K.452

This luscious quintet is scored for piano, oboe, clarinet, horn and bassoon. Mozart's magnificent orchestration of the winds with piano creates a warm and glowing texture of sound, and each instrument emerges at times for a prominent position. Cast in three movements: Largo/Allegro moderato; Larghetto; and Rondo/Allegretto. Truly one of the great works in this format and wonderful fun to practice and perform. Includes the complete clarinet solo part printed on high-quality ivory paper and a CD containing a complete performance of the quintet with soloist, then performed again minus the soloist.

Performed by Aldo Simonelli, clarinet
Accompaniment: Harriet Wingreen, piano; New Art Wind Quintet: Mel Kaplan, oboe; Tina DiDario, bassoon; Murray Panitz, flute
00400327 Book/CD Pack $14.99

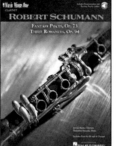

SCHUMANN – 5 FANTASY PIECES, OP. 73 AND 3 ROMANCES, OP. 94

Pieces by the great Romantic master, Robert Schumann, which offers less experienced clarinetists a slice of nineteenth-century musical perfection.

Performed by Jerome Bunke, clarinet
Accompaniment: Hidemitsu Hayashi, piano
00400316 Book/Online Audio $14.99

WEBER – CONCERTO NO. 1 IN F MINOR OP. 73 & STAMITZ: CONCERTO NO. 3 IN B-FLAT FOR CLARINET

No composer likes to write music without feeling that an artist exists both capable of, and willing to, play it to good advantage. When Carl Maria von Weber met Heinrich Joseph Baermann, one of the greatest clarinetists of the early nineteenth century, he delightedly began writing all sorts of work for him, including several chamber pieces and the two famous clarinet concerti. In his F-minor Concerto No. 1, it is clear that Weber knew the virtuosity of his player-he makes the soloist range over the entire compass of his instrument, and such quiet moments as do occur are invariably surrounded by runs, leaps and passagework of the utmost brilliance. A fantastic concerto. Also in this edition is Carl Stamitz's lovely B-flat-major concerto, a most beautiful Classical-era work. Includes a printed solo part for B-flat clarinet and audio containing a complete version with soloist, in digitally remastered stereo; then a second version of the orchestral accompaniment, minus the soloist.

Performed by Keith Dwyer, clarinet
Accompaniment: Stuttgart Festival Orchestra • Conductor: Emil Kahn
00400586 Book/Online Audio $19.99

0518